GRAPHIC SCIENCE

UNDERSTANDING VIRUSES

WITH

MAX AXIOM
SUPER SCIENTIST

4D An Augmented Reading Science Experience

by Agnieszka Biskup | illustrated by Nick Derington

Consultant:
Wade A. Bresnahan, PhD
Associate Professor
Department of Microbiology
University of Minnesota

CAPSTONE PRESS
a capstone imprint

Graphic Library is published by Capstone Press,
1710 Roe Crest Drive, North Mankato, Minnesota 56003.
www.mycapstone.com

Copyright © 2019 by Capstone Press.
All rights reserved. No part of this publication may be reproduced in whole or in part,
or stored in a retrieval system, or transmitted in any form or by any means, electronic,
mechanical, photocopying, recording, or otherwise, without written permission of the publisher.

Library of Congress Cataloging-in-Publication Data is available on the Library of Congress website.

ISBN: 978-1-5435-5877-7 (library binding)
ISBN: 978-1-5435-6032-9 (paperback)
ISBN: 978-1-5435-5887-6 (eBook PDF)

Summary: In graphic novel format, follows the adventures of Max Axiom
as he explains the science behind viruses.

Set Designer
Bob Lentz

Cover Artists
Tod G. Smith

Book Designer
Alison Thiele

Editor
Christopher Harbo

Photo Credits
Capstone Studio: Karon Dubke, 29, back cover; iStockphoto, 13

1 Ask an adult to
download the app.

 Capstone 4D
Education

2 Scan any page with the star.

3 Enjoy your cool stuff!

——— OR ———

Use this password at capstone4D.com

virus.58777

Printed in the United States of America.
PA48

TABLE OF CONTENTS

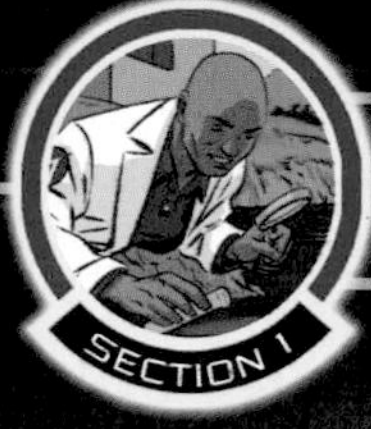
SECTION 1

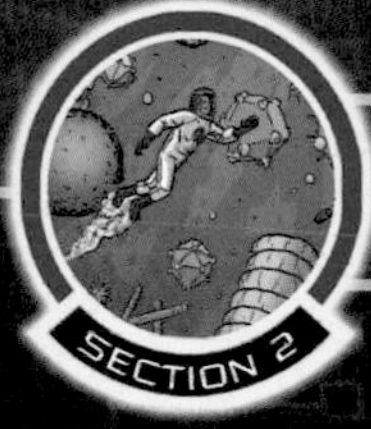
SECTION 2

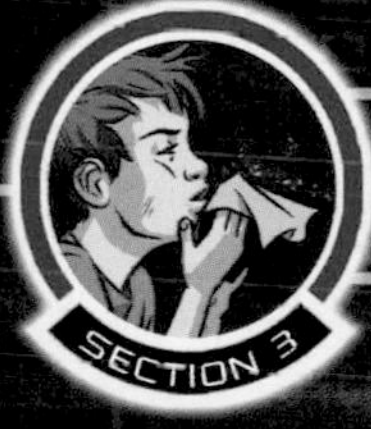
SECTION 3

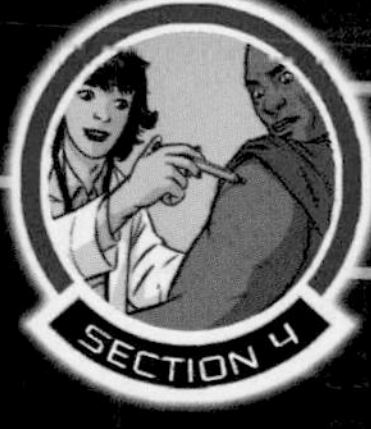
SECTION 4

SECTION 1 A MICROSCOPIC WORLD

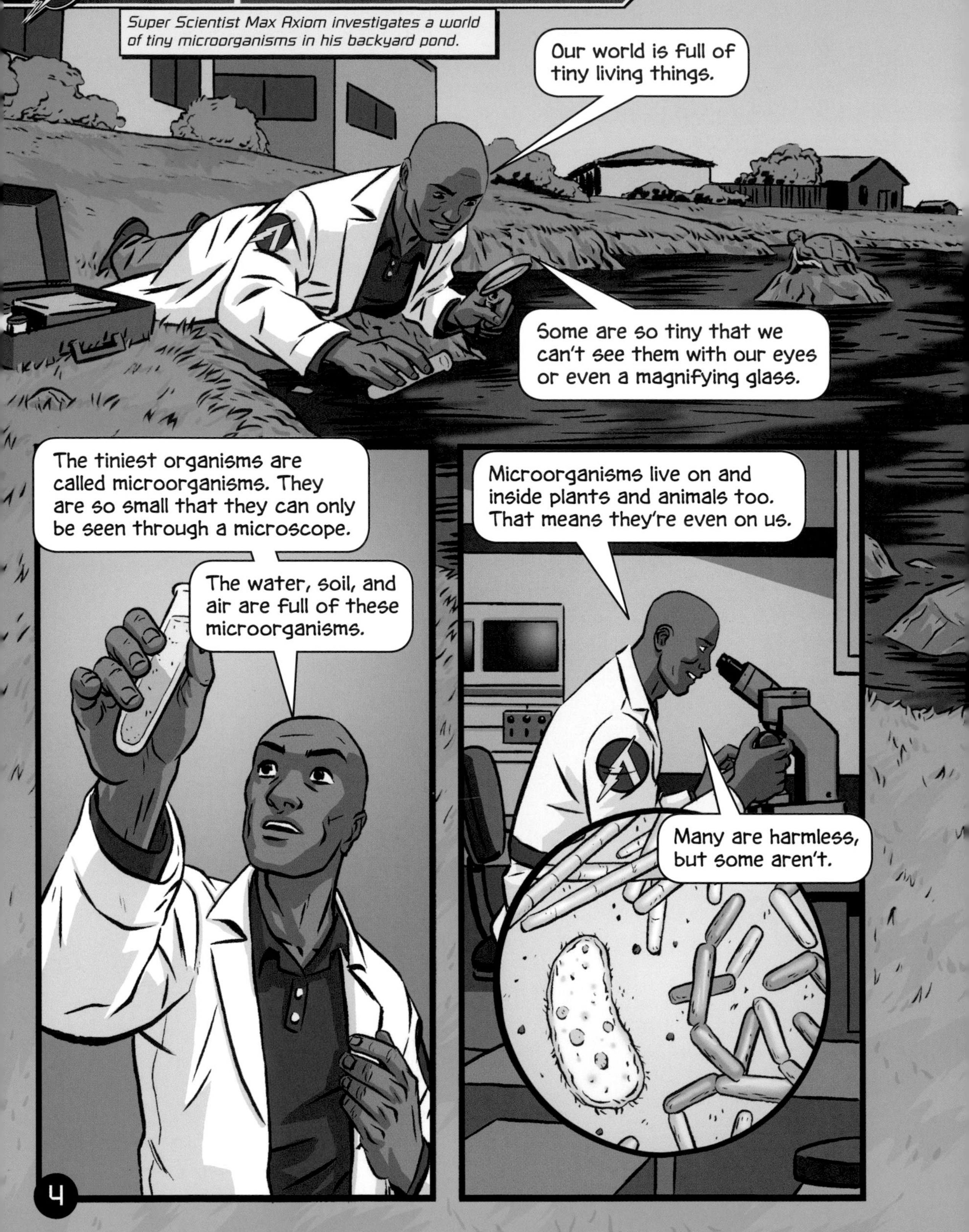
Super Scientist Max Axiom investigates a world of tiny microorganisms in his backyard pond.
Our world is full of tiny living things.
Some are so tiny that we can't see them with our eyes or even a magnifying glass.
The tiniest organisms are called microorganisms. They are so small that they can only be seen through a microscope.
The water, soil, and air are full of these microorganisms.
Microorganisms live on and inside plants and animals too. That means they're even on us.
Many are harmless, but some aren't.

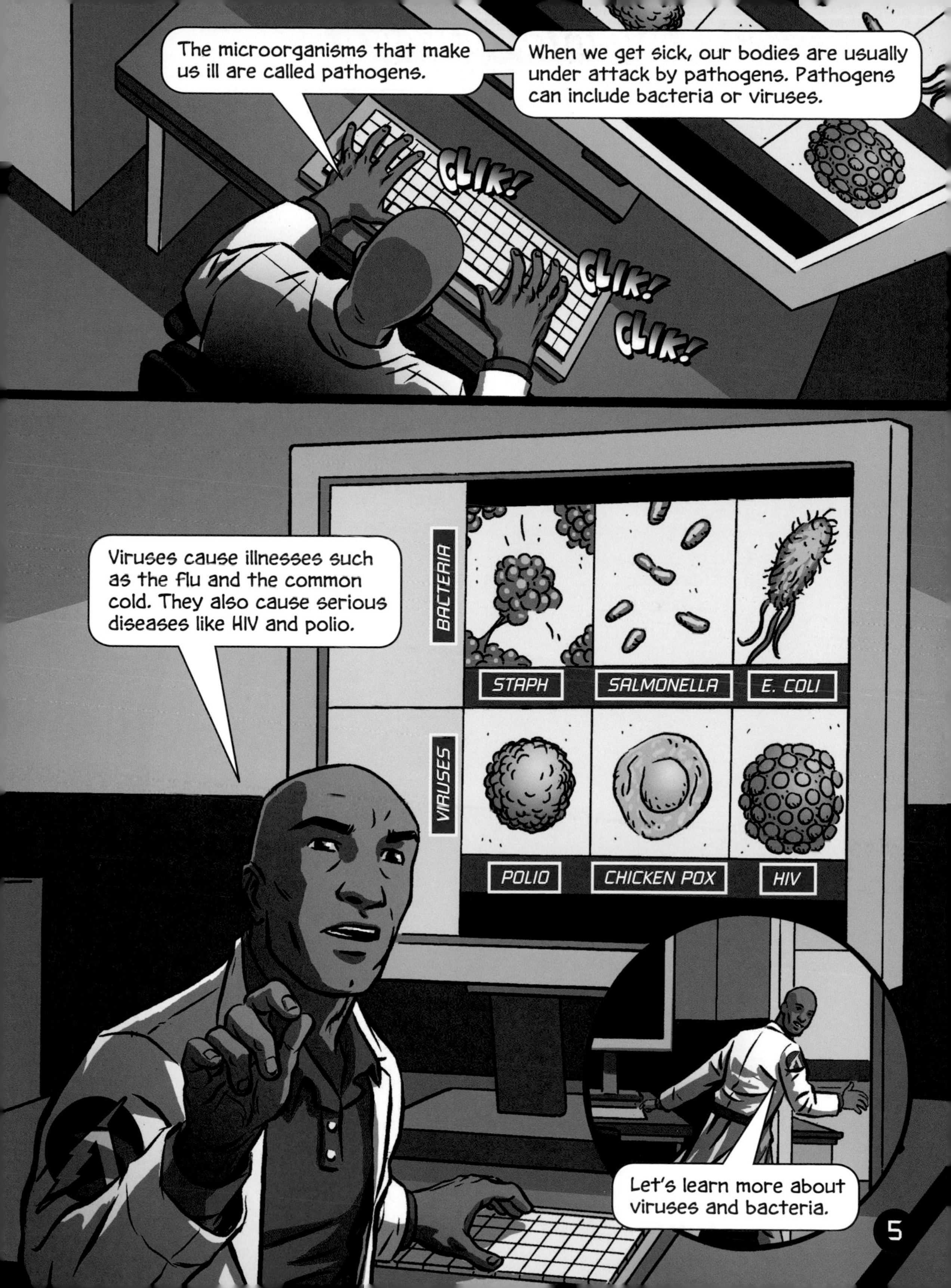
The microorganisms that make us ill are called pathogens.
When we get sick, our bodies are usually under attack by pathogens. Pathogens can include bacteria or viruses.
CLIK!
CLIK!
CLIK!
Viruses cause illnesses such as the flu and the common cold. They also cause serious diseases like HIV and polio.
BACTERIA
STAPH
SALMONELLA
E. COLI
VIRUSES
POLIO
CHICKEN POX
HIV
Let's learn more about viruses and bacteria.

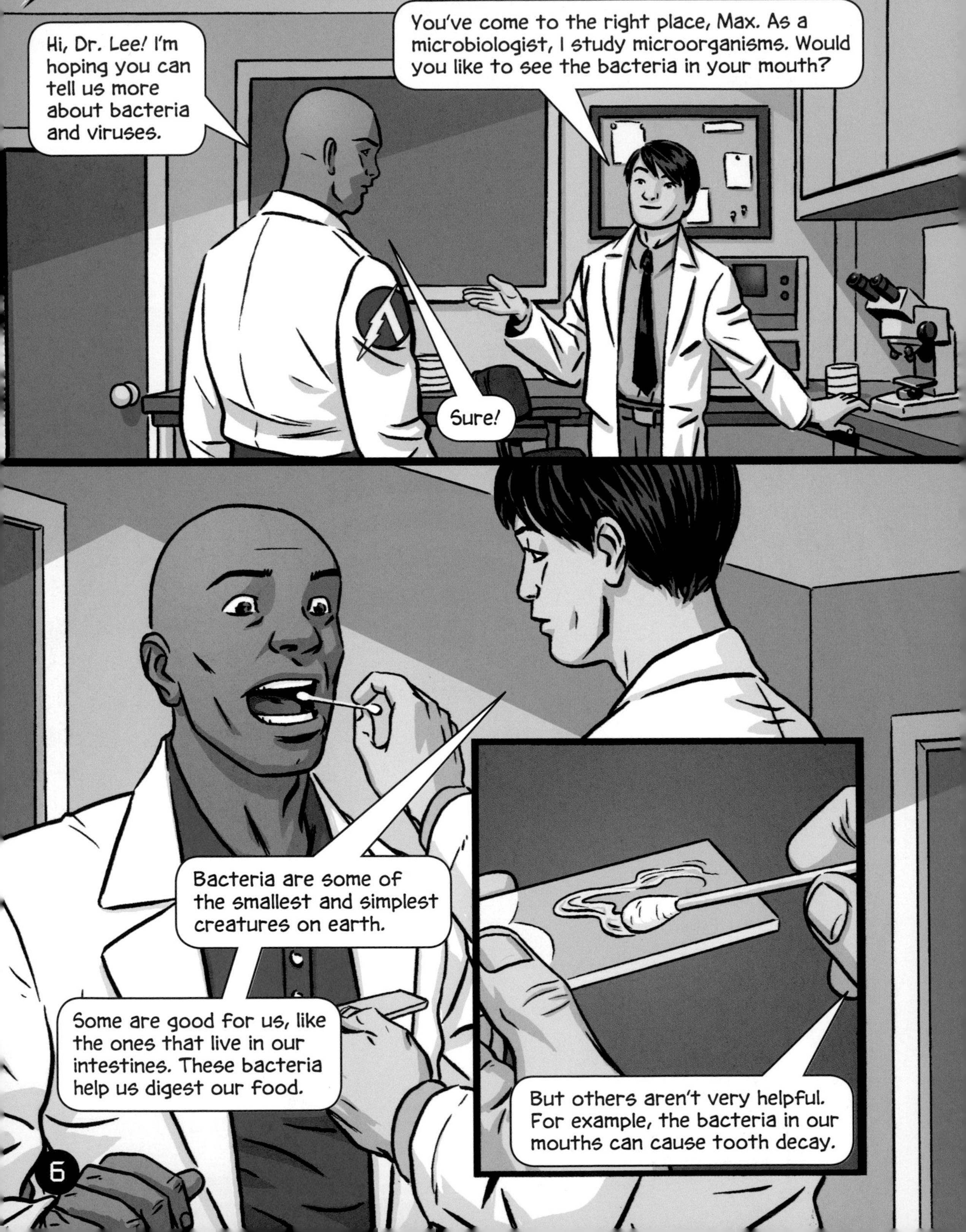
Hi, Dr. Lee! I'm hoping you can tell us more about bacteria and viruses.
You've come to the right place, Max. As a microbiologist, I study microorganisms. Would you like to see the bacteria in your mouth?
Sure!
Bacteria are some of the smallest and simplest creatures on earth.
Some are good for us, like the ones that live in our intestines. These bacteria help us digest our food.
But others aren't very helpful. For example, the bacteria in our mouths can cause tooth decay.

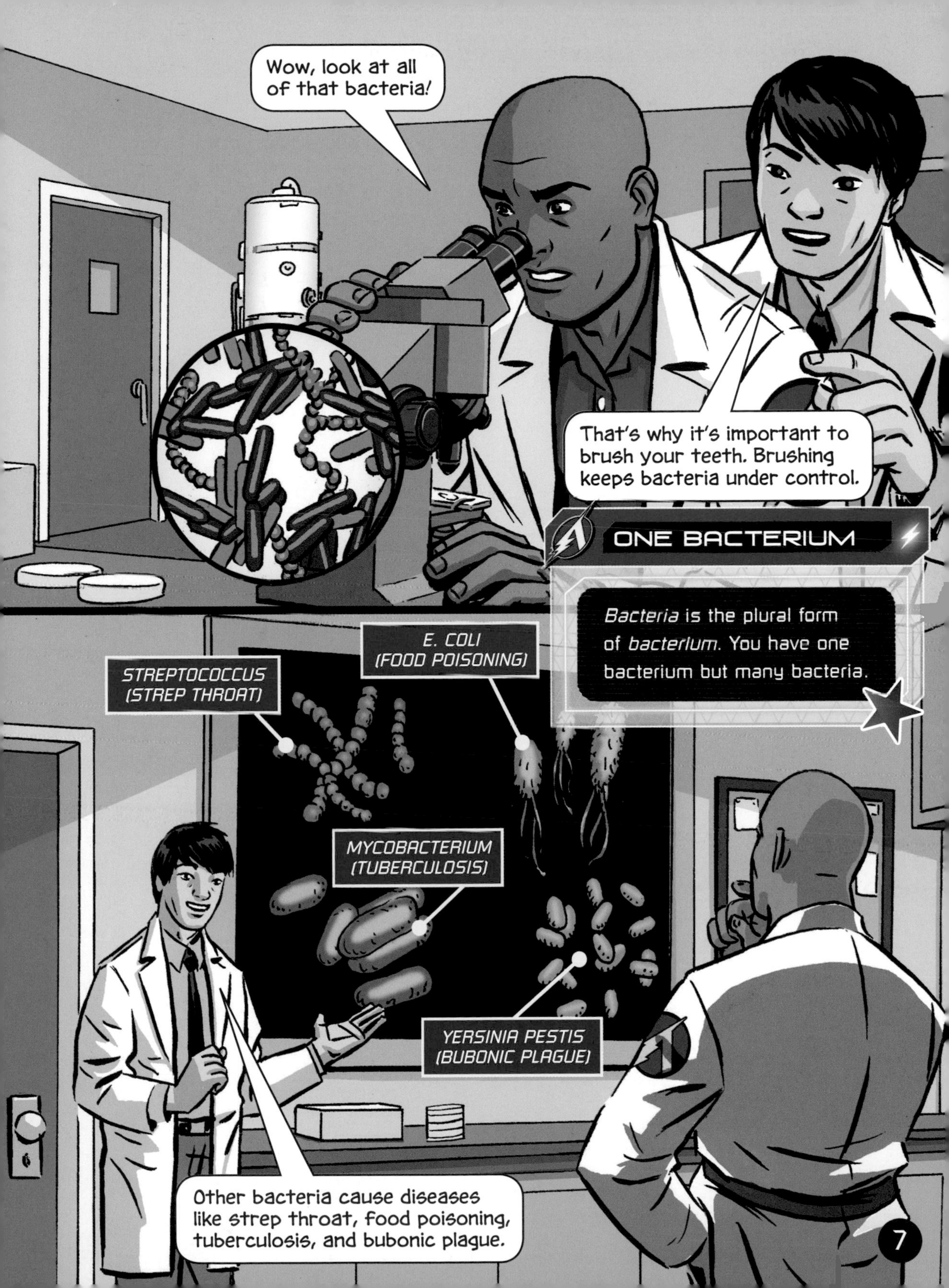

Wow, look at all of that bacteria!
That's why it's important to brush your teeth. Brushing keeps bacteria under control.
ONE BACTERIUM
Bacteria is the plural form of *bacterium*. You have one bacterium but many bacteria.
STREPTOCOCCUS (STREP THROAT)
E. COLI (FOOD POISONING)
MYCOBACTERIUM (TUBERCULOSIS)
YERSINIA PESTIS (BUBONIC PLAGUE)
Other bacteria cause diseases like strep throat, food poisoning, tuberculosis, and bubonic plague.

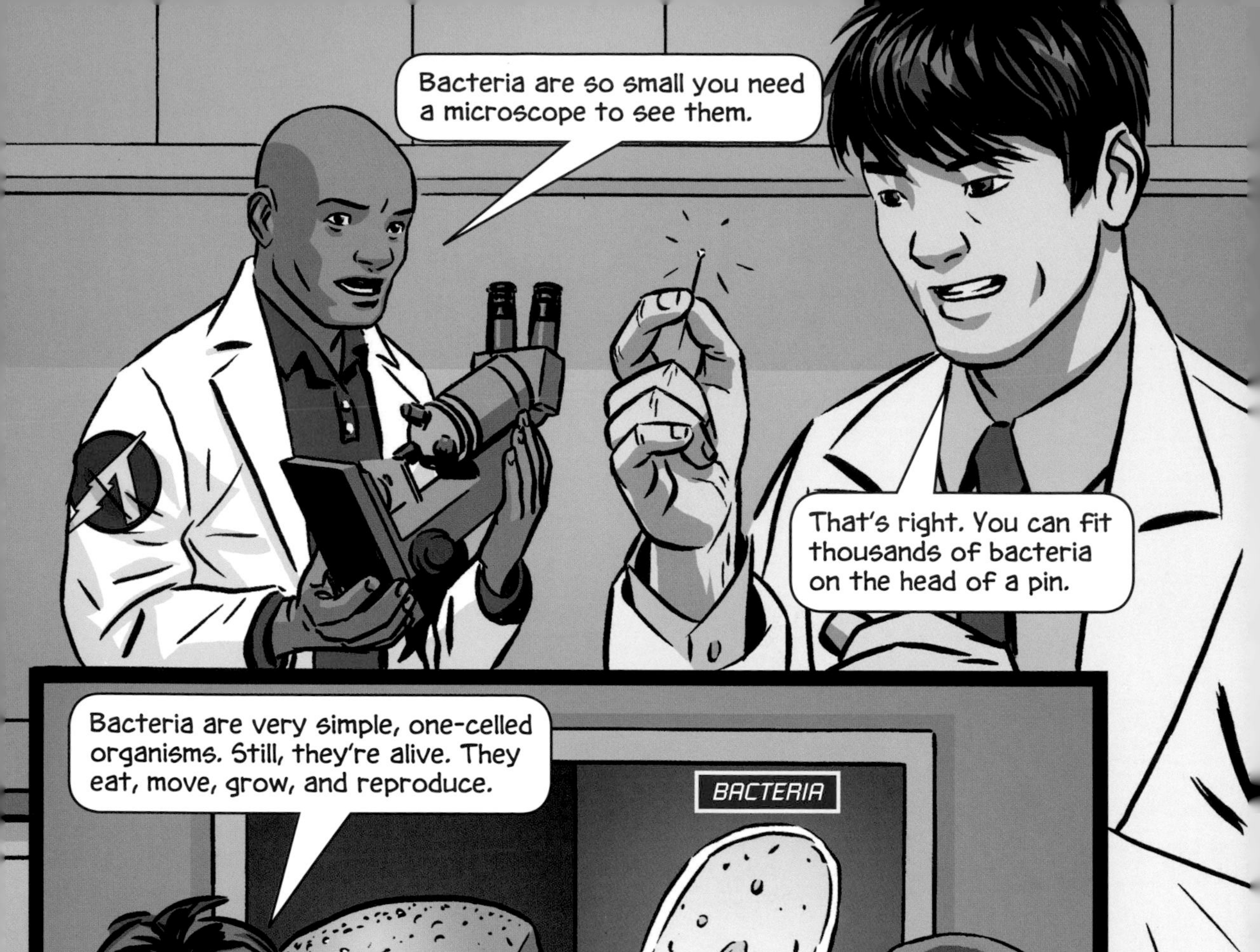
Bacteria are so small you need a microscope to see them.
That's right. You can fit thousands of bacteria on the head of a pin.
Bacteria are very simple, one-celled organisms. Still, they're alive. They eat, move, grow, and reproduce.
BACTERIA
But viruses are different.

CELLS

Cells are the basic structural unit of all living things. People are made up of trillions of cells. We have about 200 different kinds of specialized cells, including bone cells, skin cells, and blood cells.

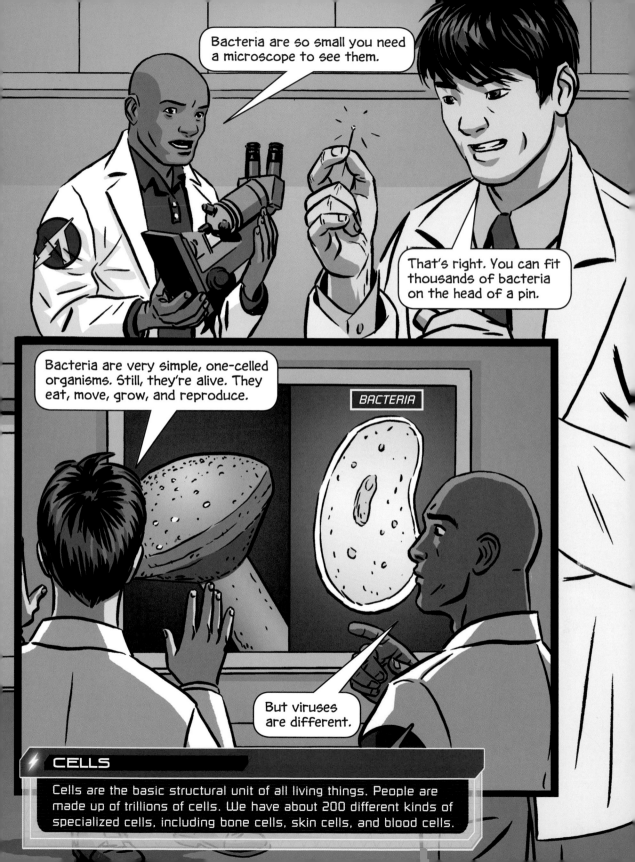

Viruses are much smaller than bacteria. They're so small that you can't see them with a regular microscope.

You need a powerful electron microscope like this one to see them.

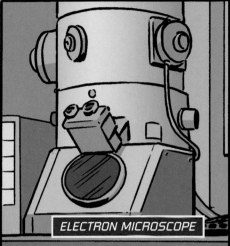

ELECTRON MICROSCOPE

A regular microscope uses light to magnify objects up to about 2,000 times.

But electron microscopes use tiny particles called electrons to magnify objects a million times and more.

Here's a virus that causes the common cold.

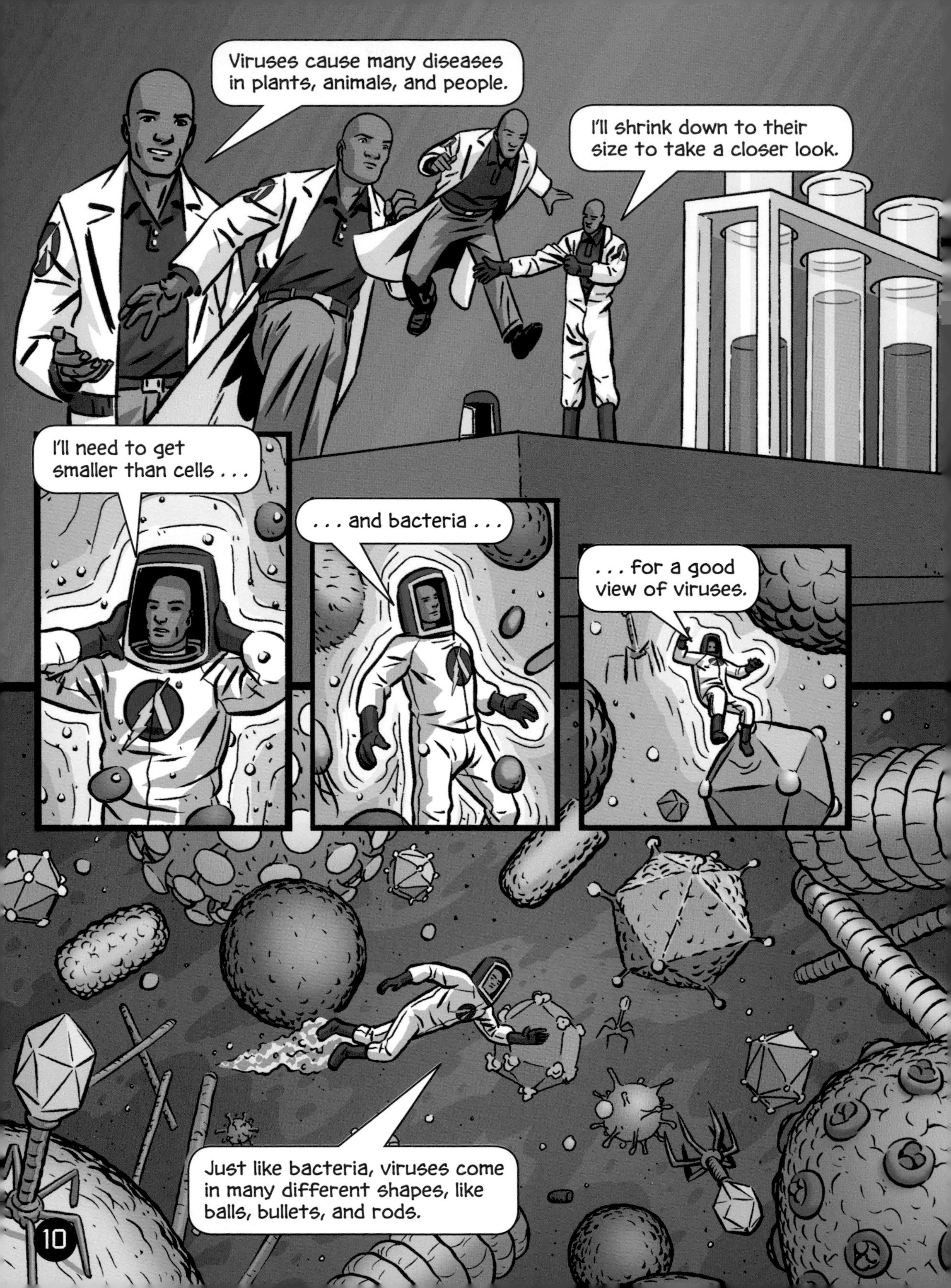
Viruses cause many diseases in plants, animals, and people.
I'll shrink down to their size to take a closer look.
I'll need to get smaller than cells . . .
. . . and bacteria . . .
. . . for a good view of viruses.
Just like bacteria, viruses come in many different shapes, like balls, bullets, and rods.

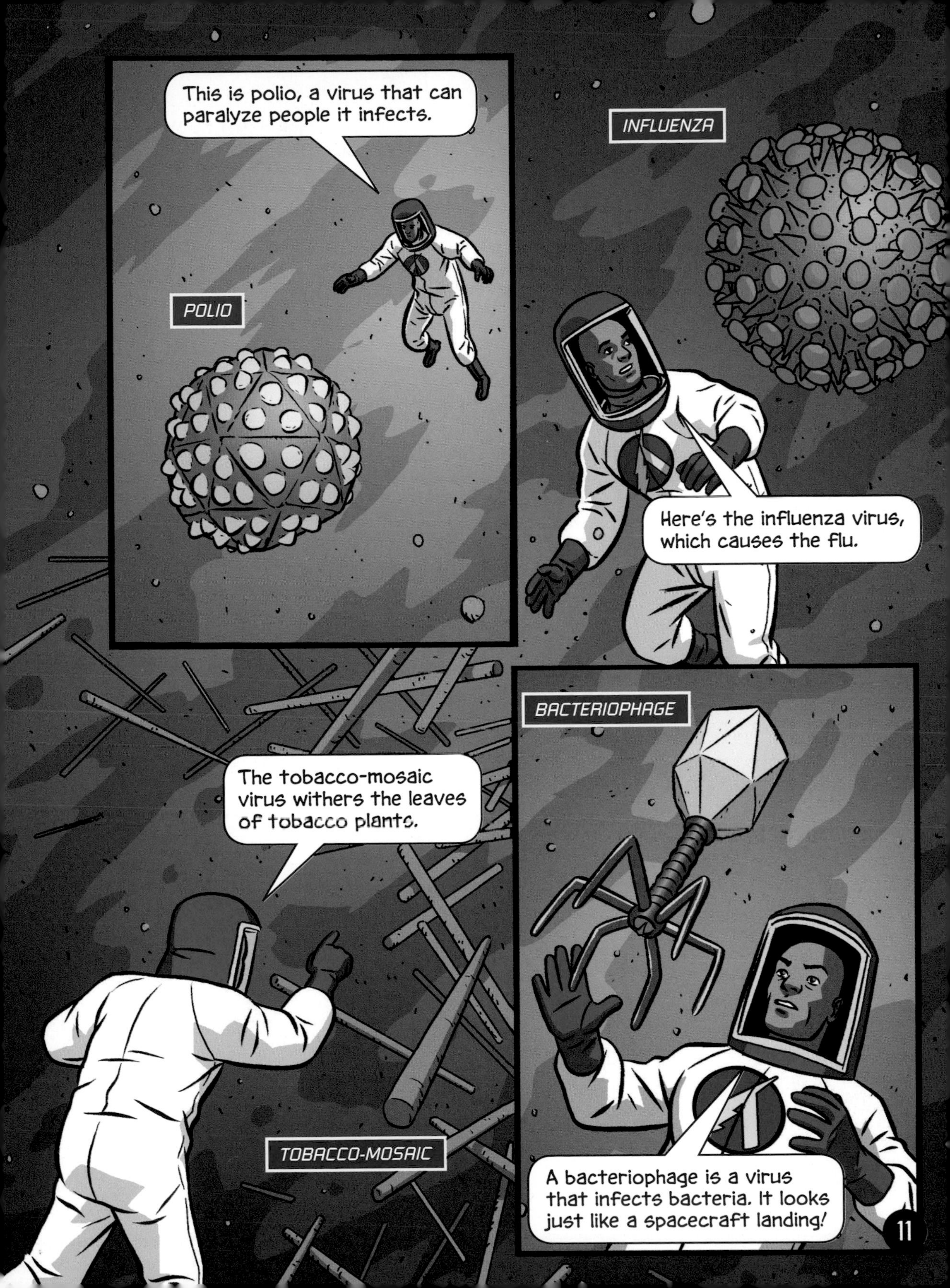
This is polio, a virus that can paralyze people it infects.
POLIO
INFLUENZA
Here's the influenza virus, which causes the flu.
The tobacco-mosaic virus withers the leaves of tobacco plants.
TOBACCO-MOSAIC
BACTERIOPHAGE
A bacteriophage is a virus that infects bacteria. It looks just like a spacecraft landing!

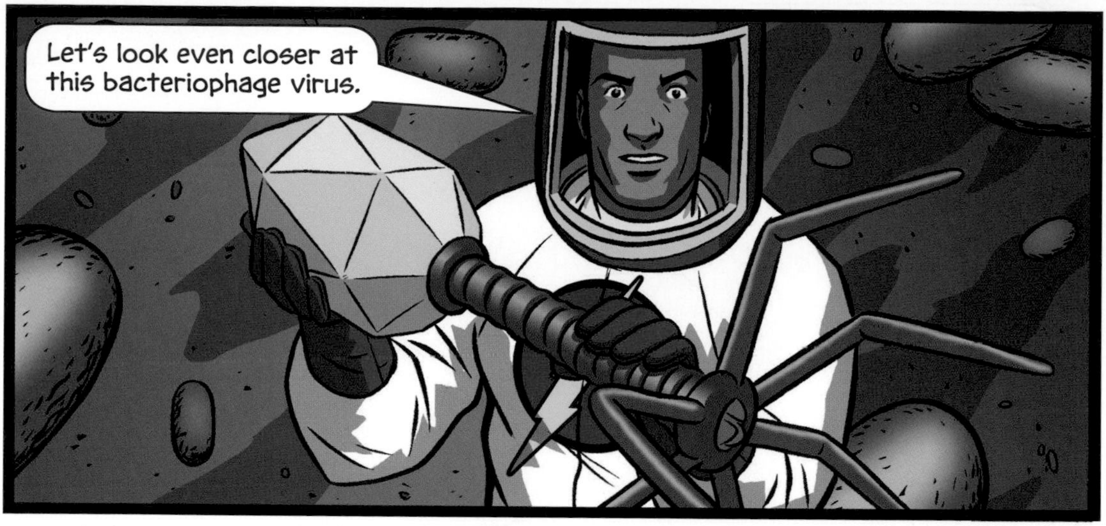
Let's look even closer at this bacteriophage virus.

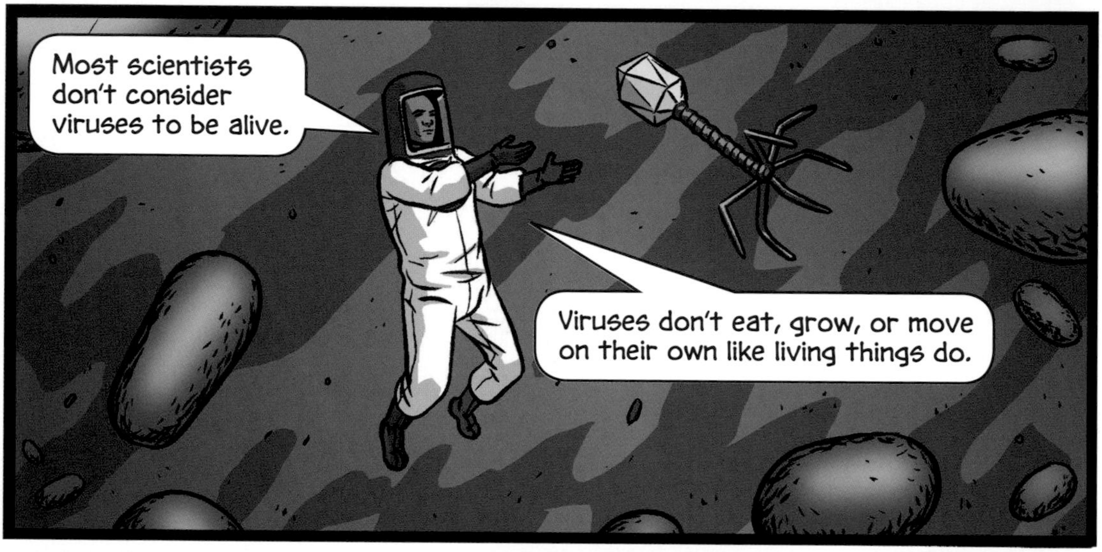
Most scientists don't consider viruses to be alive.
Viruses don't eat, grow, or move on their own like living things do.

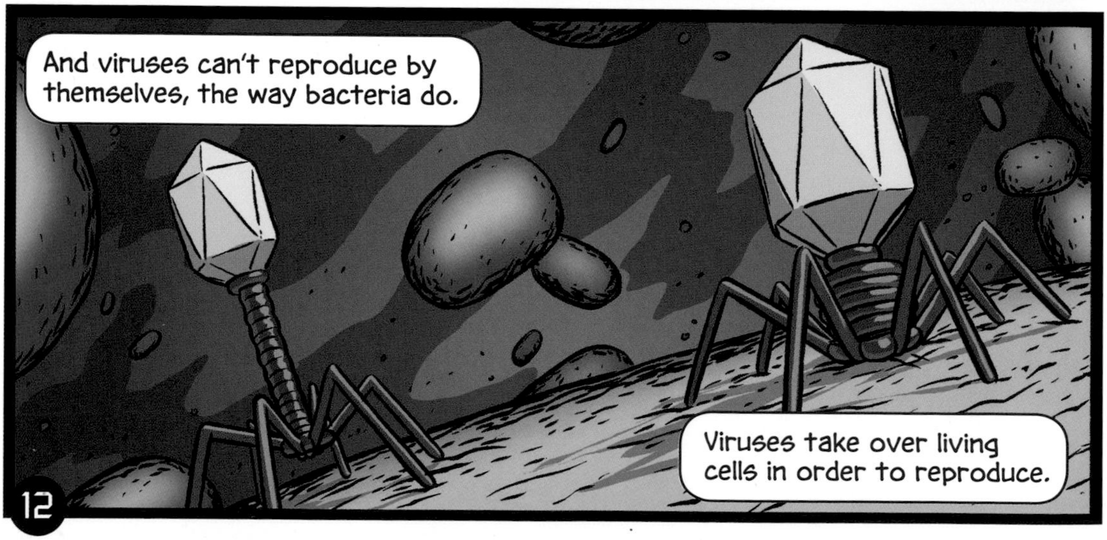
And viruses can't reproduce by themselves, the way bacteria do.
Viruses take over living cells in order to reproduce.

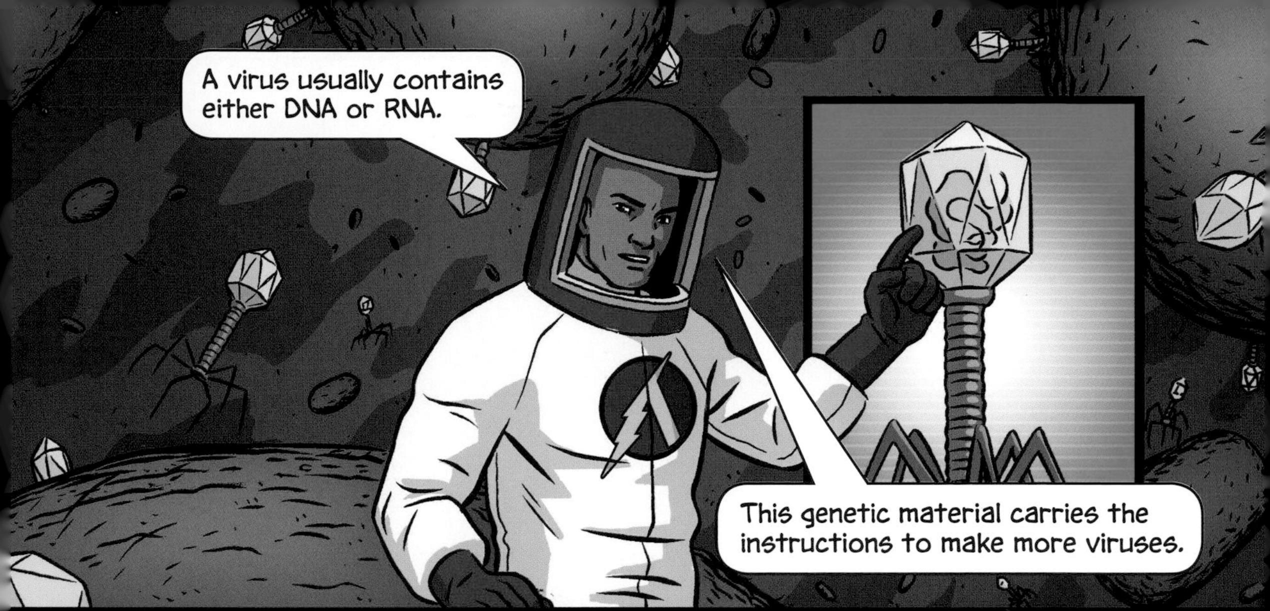
A virus usually contains either DNA or RNA.
This genetic material carries the instructions to make more viruses.

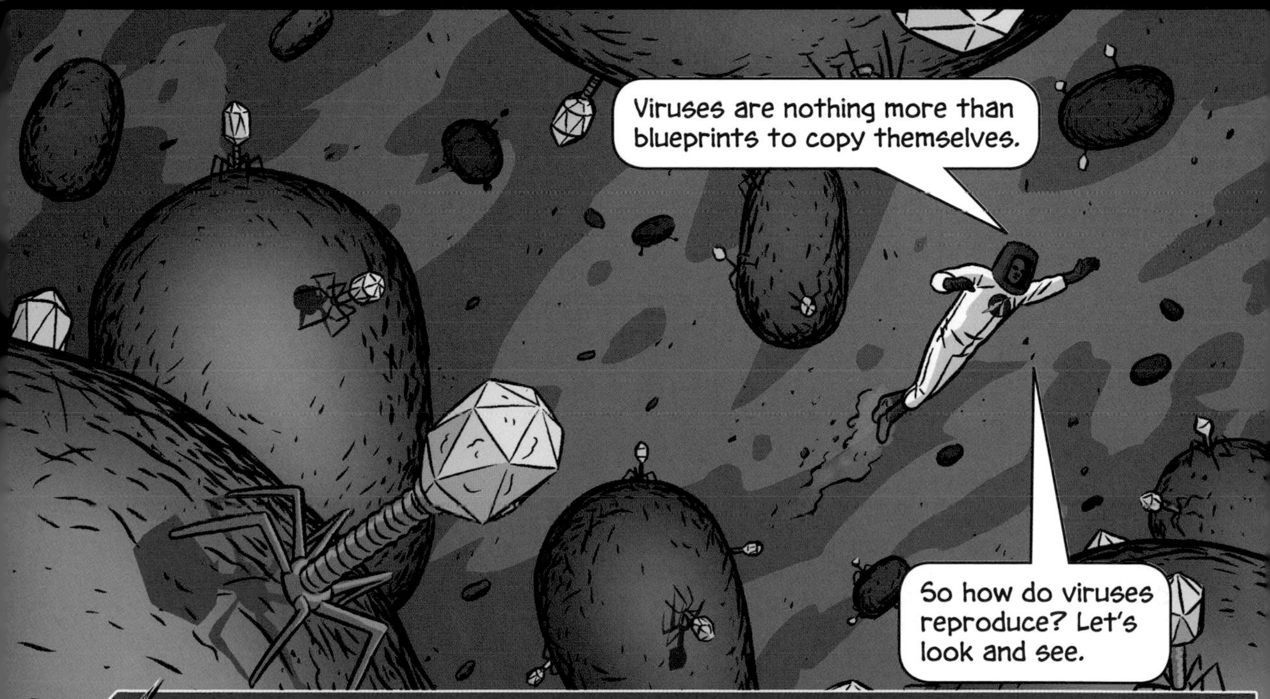
Viruses are nothing more than blueprints to copy themselves.
So how do viruses reproduce? Let's look and see.

DNA AND RNA

ACCESS GRANTED: MAX AXIOM

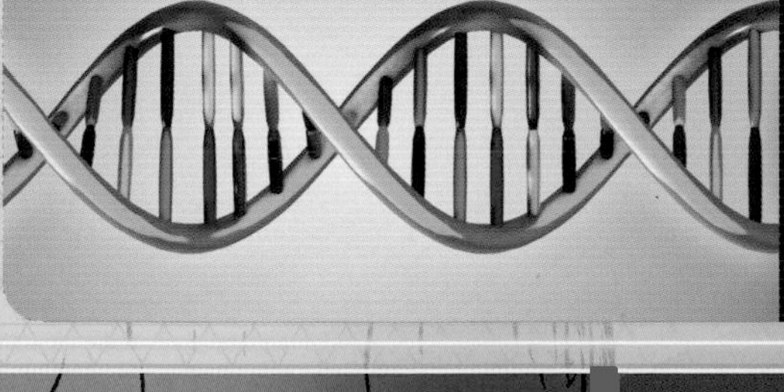

All living cells contain DNA and RNA. DNA provides all the instructions to operate and copy the cell. Cells use RNA to help translate DNA's instructions.

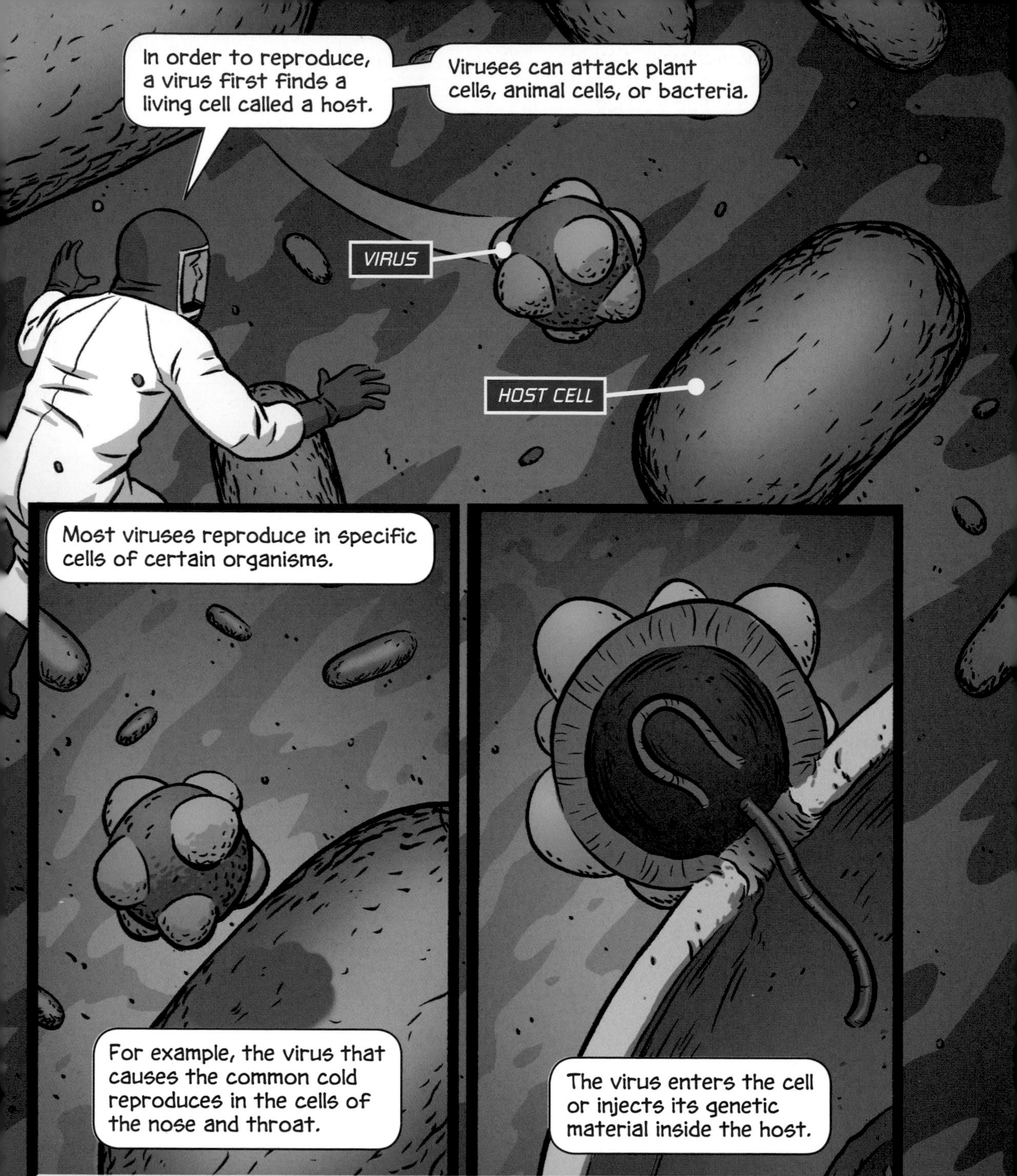
In order to reproduce, a virus first finds a living cell called a host.
Viruses can attack plant cells, animal cells, or bacteria.
VIRUS
HOST CELL
Most viruses reproduce in specific cells of certain organisms.
For example, the virus that causes the common cold reproduces in the cells of the nose and throat.
The virus enters the cell or injects its genetic material inside the host.

DORMANT VIRUSES

Some viruses can live in cells without harming them. They insert their genetic material, but no viruses are made immediately. They can stay inactive in the cell for long periods of time, until some change or stress activates them.

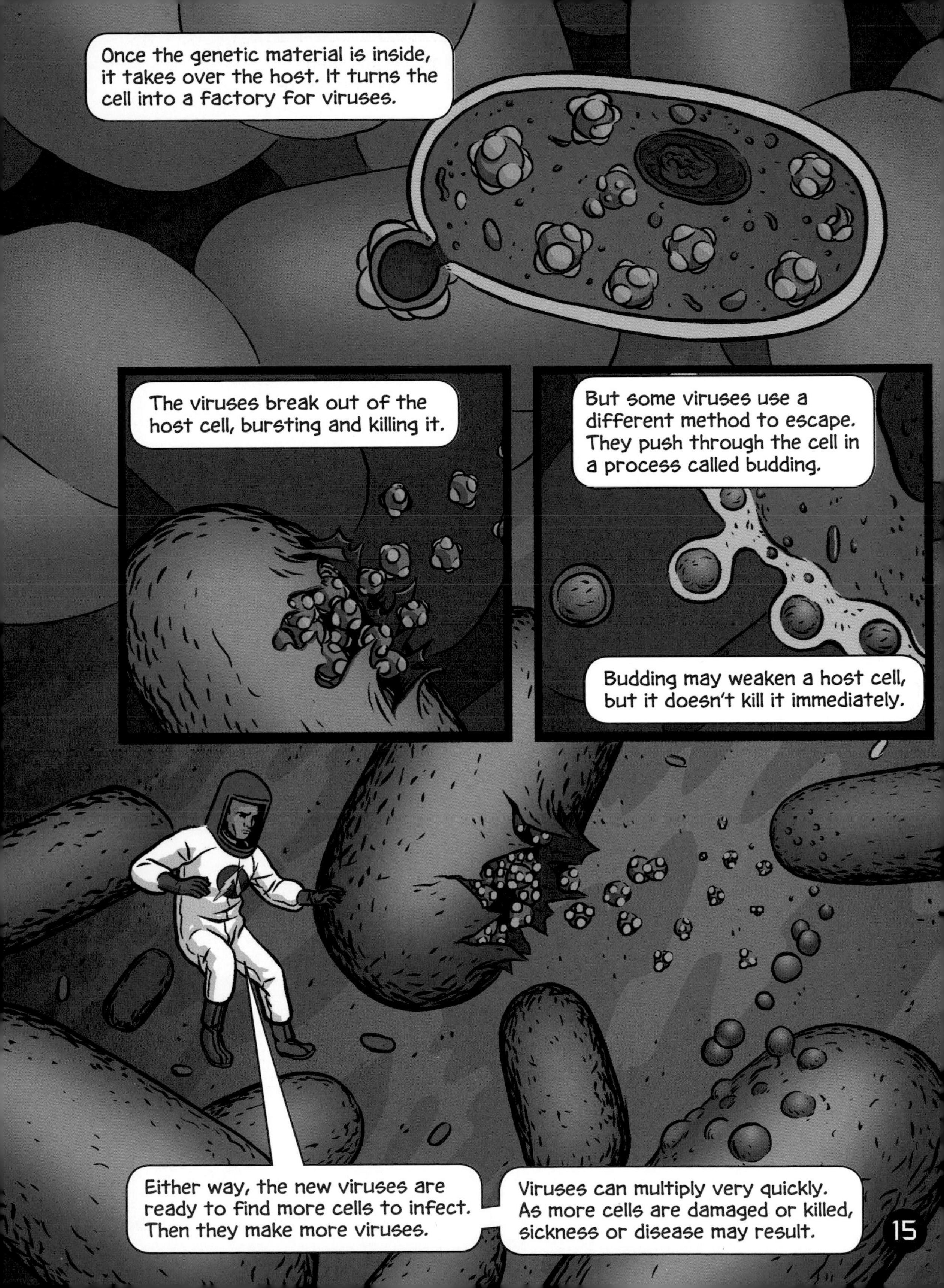

Once the genetic material is inside, it takes over the host. It turns the cell into a factory for viruses.
The viruses break out of the host cell, bursting and killing it.
But some viruses use a different method to escape. They push through the cell in a process called budding.
Budding may weaken a host cell, but it doesn't kill it immediately.
Either way, the new viruses are ready to find more cells to infect. Then they make more viruses.
Viruses can multiply very quickly. As more cells are damaged or killed, sickness or disease may result.

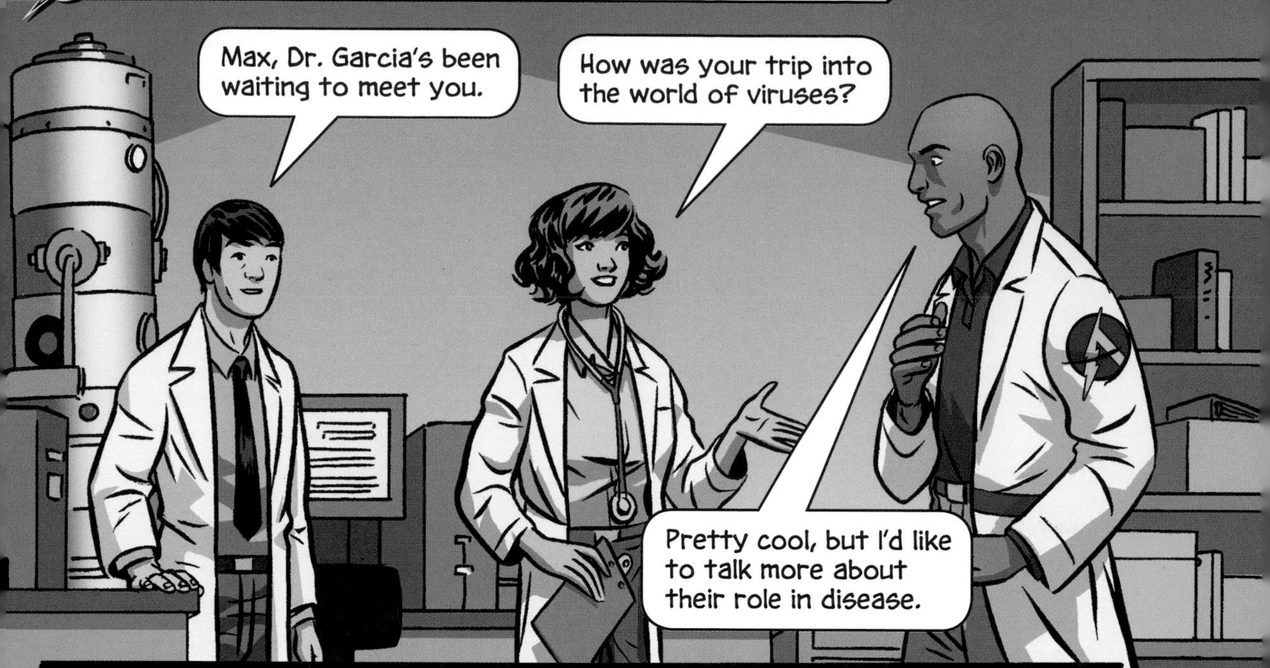
Max, Dr. Garcia's been waiting to meet you.
How was your trip into the world of viruses?
Pretty cool, but I'd like to talk more about their role in disease.

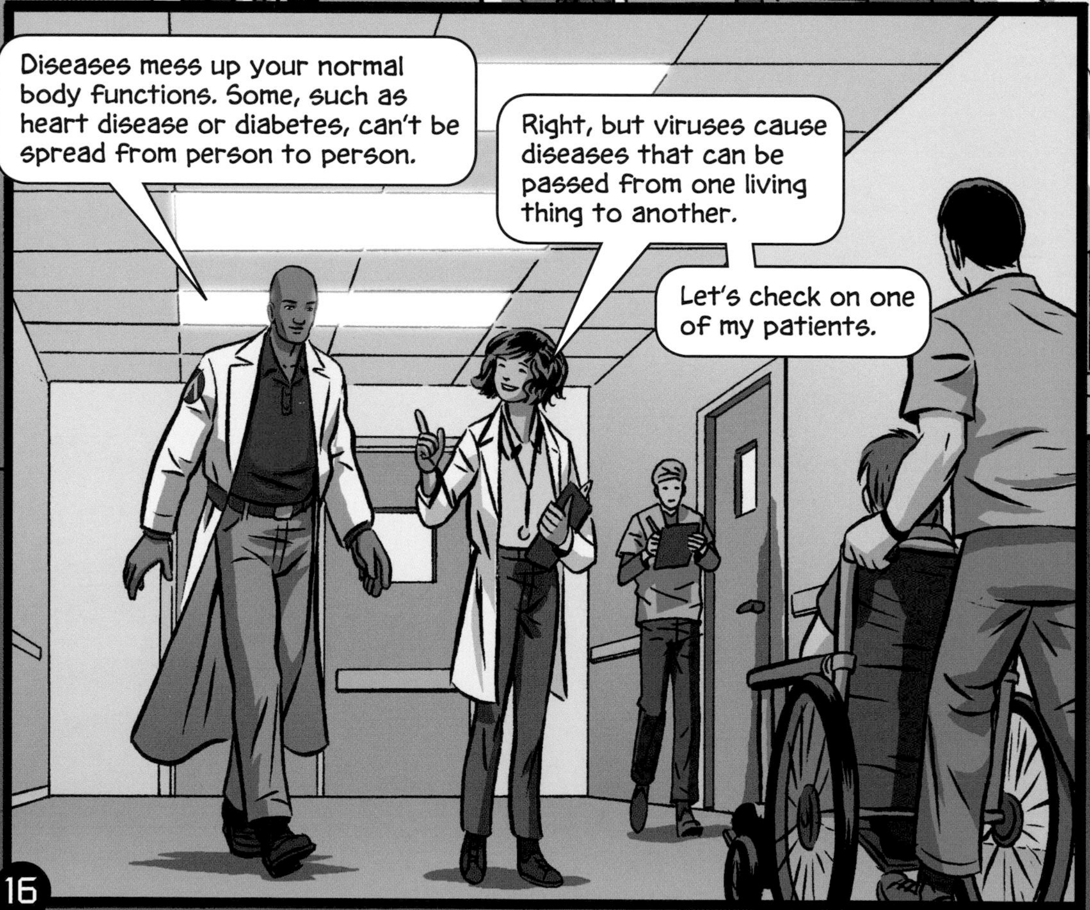
Diseases mess up your normal body functions. Some, such as heart disease or diabetes, can't be spread from person to person.
Right, but viruses cause diseases that can be passed from one living thing to another.
Let's check on one of my patients.

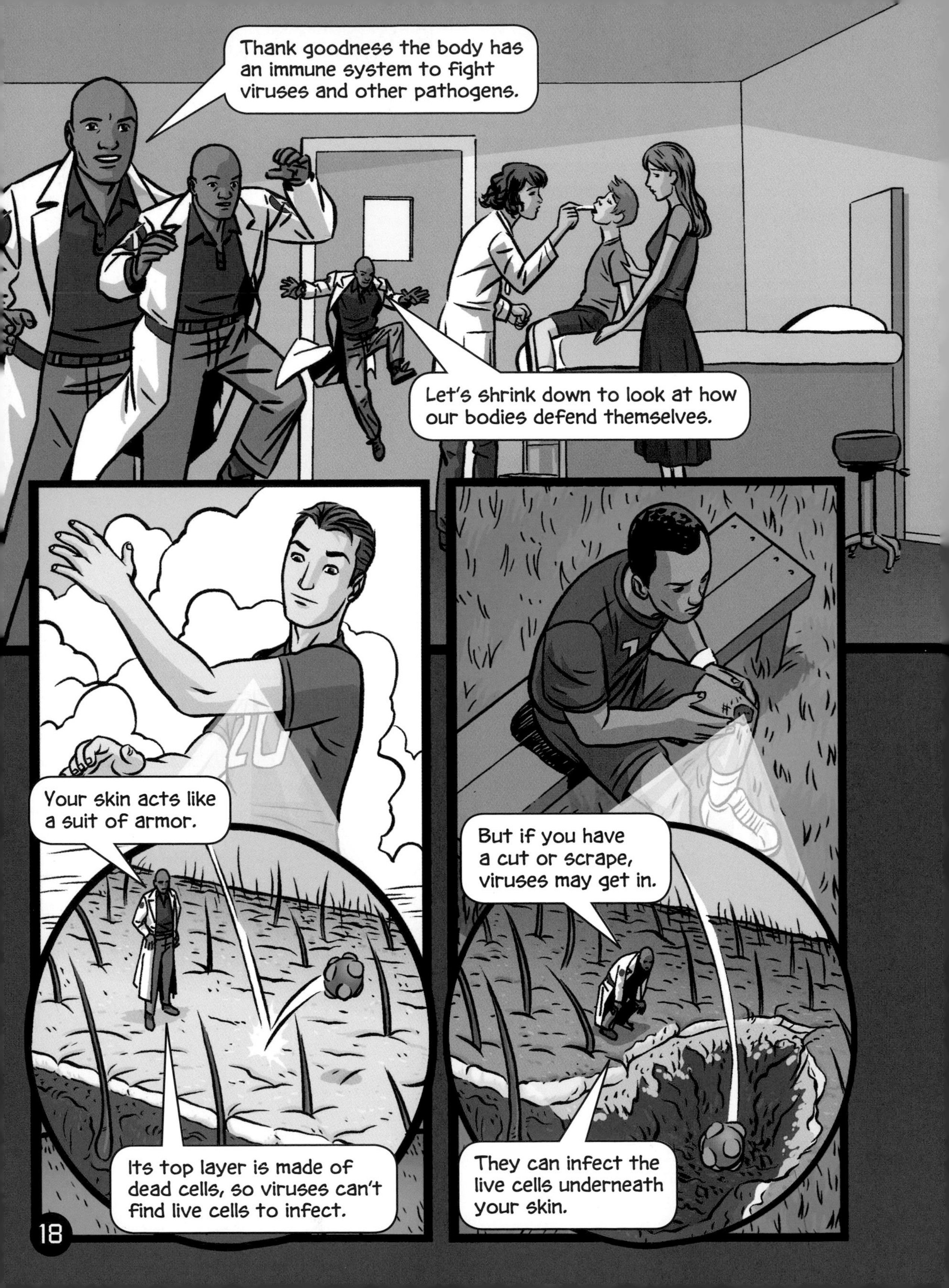
Thank goodness the body has an immune system to fight viruses and other pathogens.
Let's shrink down to look at how our bodies defend themselves.
Your skin acts like a suit of armor.
Its top layer is made of dead cells, so viruses can't find live cells to infect.
But if you have a cut or scrape, viruses may get in.
They can infect the live cells underneath your skin.

But our bodies have yet another defense against viruses.
Let's enter the bloodstream for a closer look at a cell under attack.
RED BLOOD CELLS
We fight back with white blood cells in our bloodstream.
When our cells are under attack, white blood cells come to their aid.
White blood cells can kill the pathogen or the infected cell.
WHITE BLOOD CELL

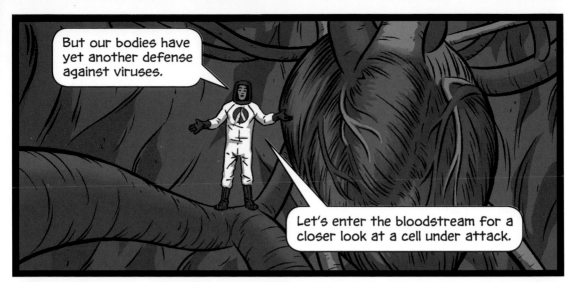

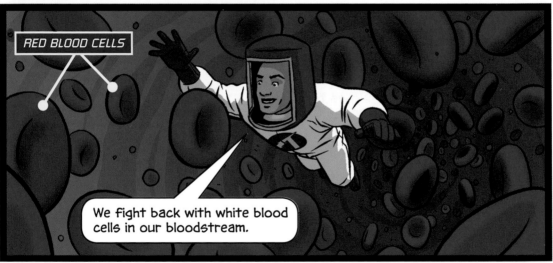

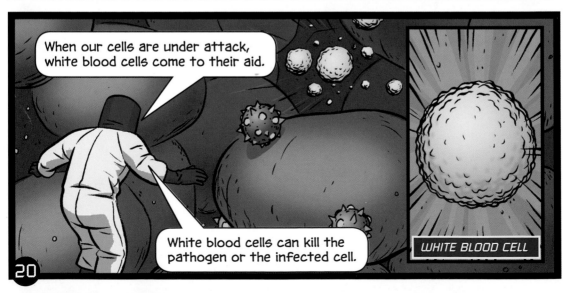

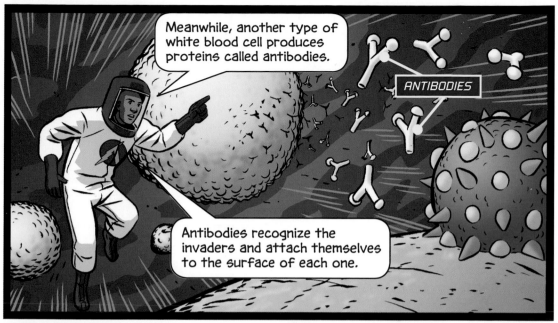

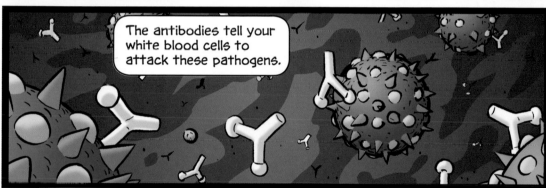

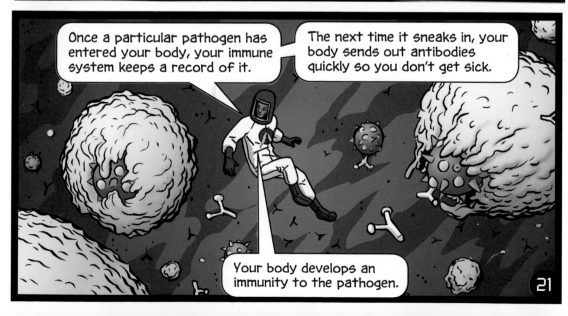

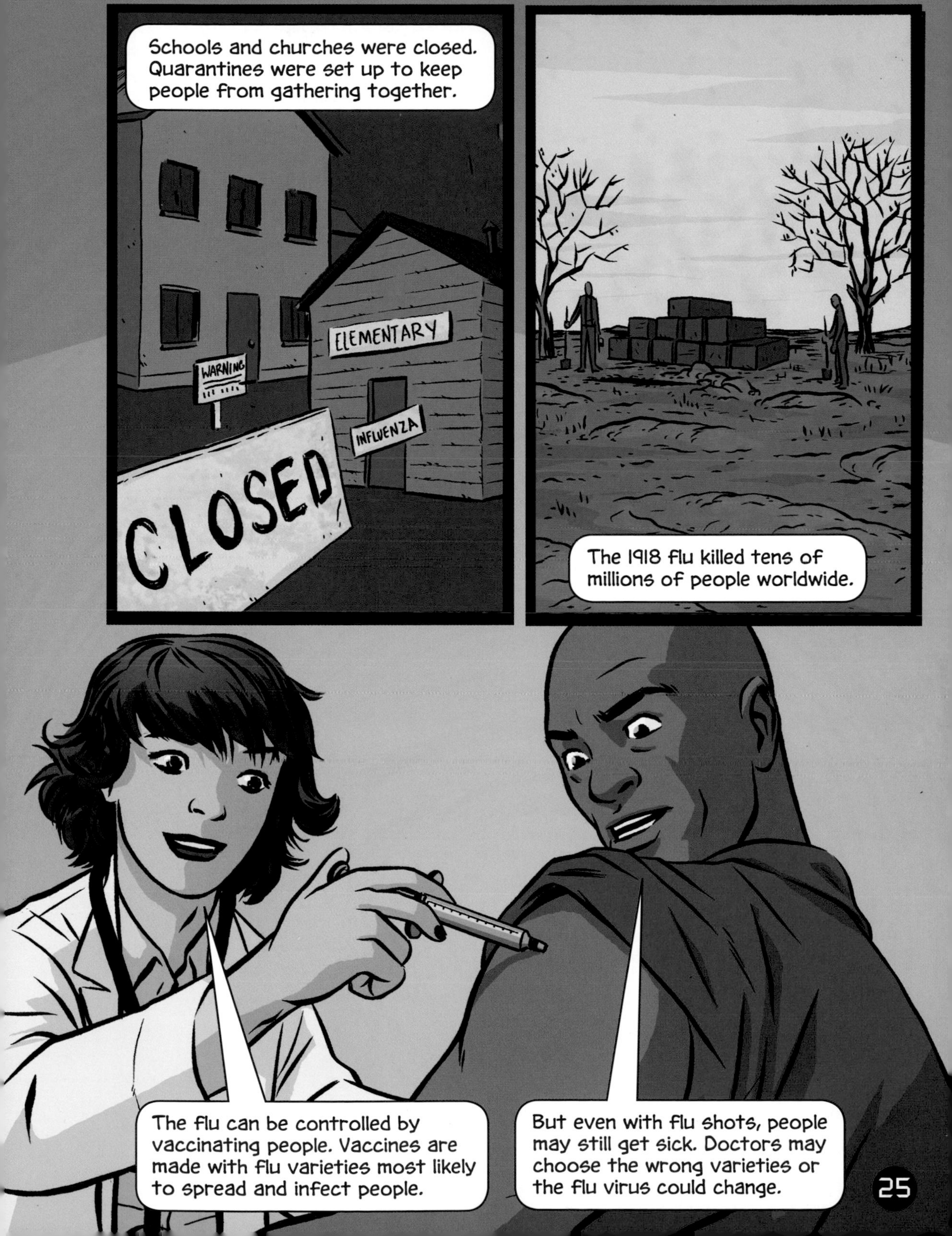
Schools and churches were closed. Quarantines were set up to keep people from gathering together.
WARNING
ELEMENTARY
INFLUENZA
CLOSED
The 1918 flu killed tens of millions of people worldwide.
The flu can be controlled by vaccinating people. Vaccines are made with flu varieties most likely to spread and infect people.
But even with flu shots, people may still get sick. Doctors may choose the wrong varieties or the flu virus could change.

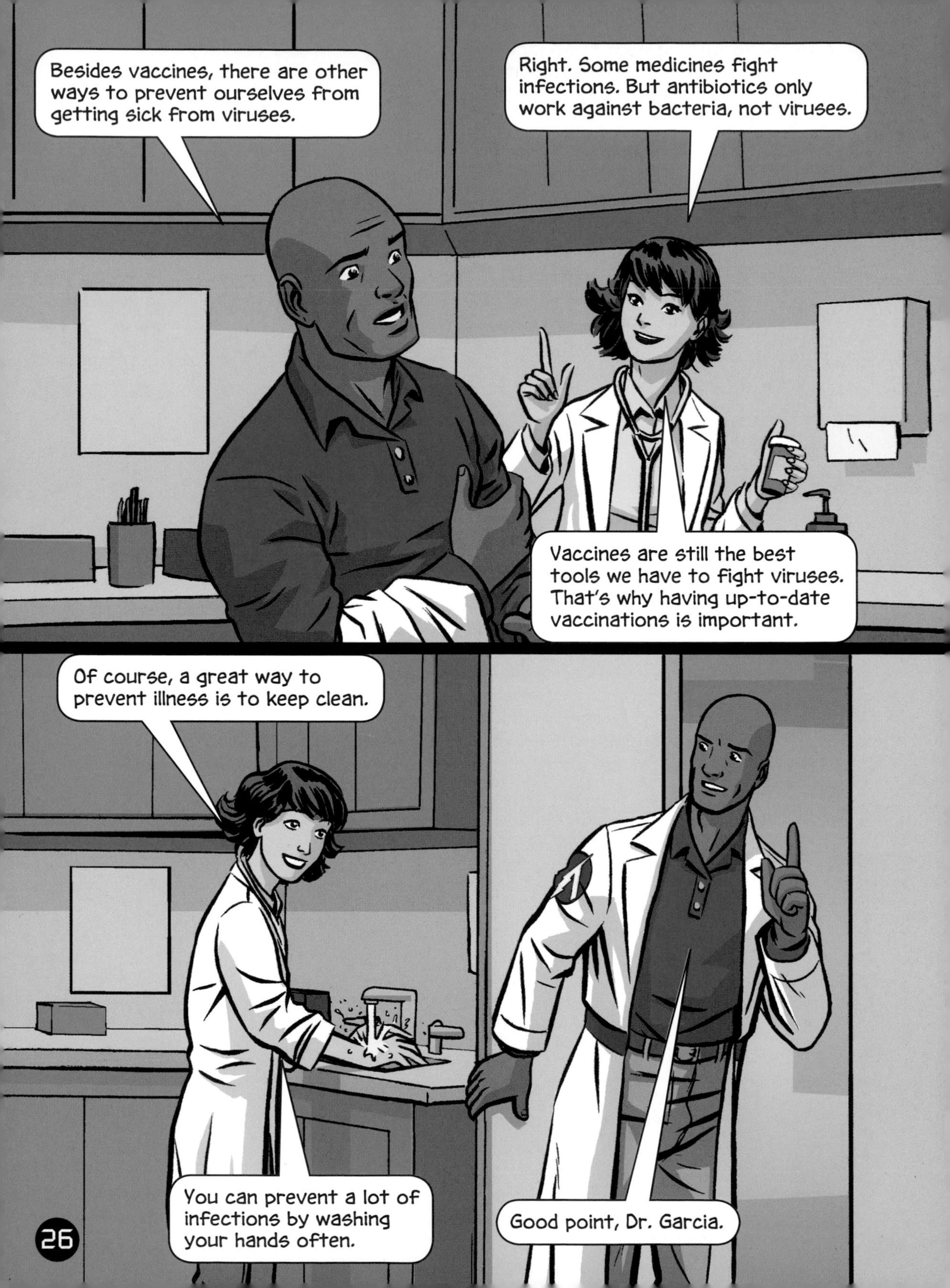
Besides vaccines, there are other ways to prevent ourselves from getting sick from viruses.
Right. Some medicines fight infections. But antibiotics only work against bacteria, not viruses.
Vaccines are still the best tools we have to fight viruses. That's why having up-to-date vaccinations is important.
Of course, a great way to prevent illness is to keep clean.
You can prevent a lot of infections by washing your hands often.
Good point, Dr. Garcia.

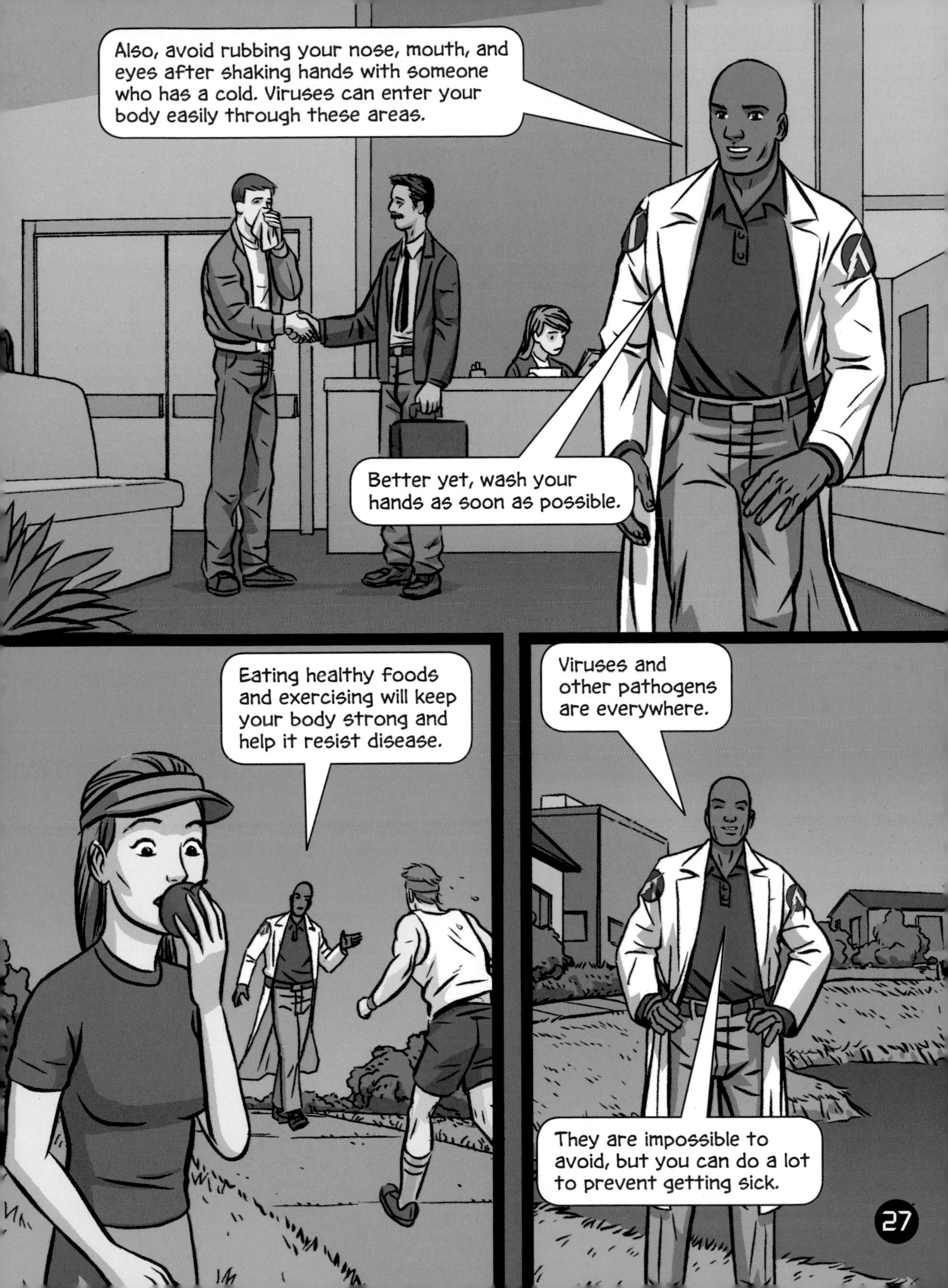
Also, avoid rubbing your nose, mouth, and eyes after shaking hands with someone who has a cold. Viruses can enter your body easily through these areas.
Better yet, wash your hands as soon as possible.
Eating healthy foods and exercising will keep your body strong and help it resist disease.
Viruses and other pathogens are everywhere.
They are impossible to avoid, but you can do a lot to prevent getting sick.

MORE ABOUT VIRUSES

We usually only hear about bad bacteria and ways to get rid of them. But only a small percentage of bacteria is truly harmful. In fact, many bacteria are very helpful. Without bacteria, we couldn't turn milk into cheese, sour cream, or yogurt. We use bacteria to help produce antibiotics and other medicines. Bacteria are even used to clean up oil spills.

Viruses can cause the colorful streaks and patterns you see in the petals of some tulips.

Having a fever is not always bad. Many viruses and bacteria don't grow as well when your body temperature rises above normal. A fever is often just your body trying to defend itself against infection.

Animals get sick from viruses too. That's why it's important to get your pets vaccinated against rabies, distemper, and other diseases.

Genetic mutations can sometimes allow a virus to jump from animals to humans. For example, pigs and birds can get the flu. In some cases, they can pass it on to people.

The virus known as HIV causes the serious disease called AIDS. HIV attacks the immune system, reducing its ability to fight off disease. HIV is spread only through direct contact with an infected person's bodily fluids, such as blood. Right now, there is no cure or vaccine for HIV infection or AIDS. Some medications, however, can help people with HIV live longer lives.

Vaccines aren't just for viruses. They're also used to protect people against some diseases caused by bacteria. Scientists have made vaccines for bacteria such as diphtheria, pertussis (whooping cough), and tetanus.

A computer virus is a computer program that copies itself. It is passed between computers like a virus is passed from person to person. And just like a regular virus, computer viruses can be harmful. They can delete data and steal personal information.

BUILD A BACTERIOPHAGE

Learn about the parts of a
bacteriophage virus by building
your very own model.

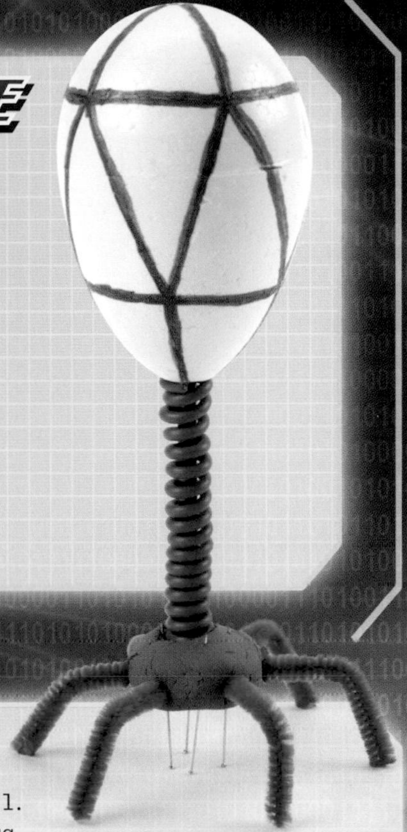

WHAT YOU NEED:

- marker
- foam egg
- large nail
- insulated wire
- wire cutter
- modeling clay
- pipe cleaner
- 4 pins

WHAT YOU DO:

1. Look at the illustration of a bacteriophage on page 11.
   Use a marker to draw triangle shapes on the foam egg
   to create the head of the bacteriophage.

2. Carefully push the point of the nail into the narrow end of the foam egg.

3. Tightly wrap insulated wire around the full length of the nail. Use the
   wire cutter to snip off any extra wire. The wire-wrapped nail is the sheathed
   tail of the bacteriophage.

4. Roll the modeling clay into a small ball. Press the head of the nail into the clay ball.

5. Squash the clay ball into a thick disc shape that holds the nail firmly. The squashed
   modeling clay represents the bacteriophage's baseplate.

6. Cut the three pipe cleaners in half with the wire cutter. Insert the pipe cleaner pieces
   into the modeling clay, spacing them evenly all the way around its edge. Bend the
   pipe cleaners into right angles to represent the tail fibers of the bacteriophage.

7. Insert four pins into the underside of the modeling clay to represent the
   bacteriophage's tail pins. Your virus model is now complete!

DISCUSSION QUESTIONS

1. Compare and contrast viruses and bacteria. How are they alike and how are they different?

2. What is the difference between a regular microscope and an electron microscope? Which one would you need to use to see a virus and why?

3. In order to reproduce, a virus attacks a living host cell. What are two ways that viruses can damage or kill the host cell?

4. If a person is exposed to a virus, how does the body defend itself to keep the virus from infecting cells?

WRITING PROMPTS

1. Viruses and bacteria can both make you sick. Based on what you've read, make one list of illnesses and diseases caused by viruses and a list of those caused by bacteria.

2. If you could make a vaccine that would remove one disease from the world, which disease would you get rid of? Write a paragraph explaining how removing the disease would make the world better.

3. Some viruses look like spaceships and others look like spiky balls. Design a virus of your very own and draw a picture of it. Then give your virus a name and write a short paragraph about it.

4. Every year cold and flu viruses spread from person to person in your school. Write a short paragraph explaining the measures you and your friends can take to prevent these viruses from spreading.

TAKE A QUIZ!

GLOSSARY

bacteria (bak-TIR-ee-uh)—one-celled, tiny organisms that can be found throughout nature; many bacteria are useful, but some cause disease

DNA (dee-en-AY)—the molecule that carries all of the instructions to make a living thing and keep it working

HIV (AYCH-ie-vee)—the virus that causes AIDS; HIV attacks the body's immune system, making patients more likely to get other illnesses

immune system (i-MYOON SISS-tuhm)—the part of the body that protects against germs and diseases

influenza (in-floo-EN-zuh)—an illness that is like a bad cold with fever and muscle pain; a virus causes influenza

mutation (myoo-TAY-shuhn)—a permanent change in nature, form, or quality; when viruses mutate they sometimes become stronger and more dangerous

pathogen (PATH-uh-juhn)—a germ that causes diseases

polio (POH-lee-oh)—an infectious viral disease that attacks the brain and spinal cord

quarantine (KWOR-uhn-teen)—limiting or forbidding the movement of people to prevent the spread of disease

RNA (AHR-en-ay)—a molecule found in all cells that carries instructions for making proteins

vaccine (vak-SEEN)—a substance used to protect people and animals against disease

READ MORE

Bozzone, Donna M. *Understanding Microbes.* Heredity and Genetics. New York: Enslow Publishing, 2019.

Halvorson, Karin. *Inside Your Germs.* Super Simple Body. Minneapolis: Abdo Publishing, 2016.

Hand, Carol. *The Gross Science of Germs All Around You.* Way Gross Science. New York: Rosen Central, 2019.

Marsico, Katie. *Look Out for Germs!* My Healthy Habits. Ann Arbor, Mich.: Cherry Lake Publishing, 2019.

INTERNET SITES

Use Facthound to find Internet sites related to this book.

Visit *www.facthound.com*

Just type in 9781543558777 and go!

Check out projects, games and lots more at
www.capstonekids.com

INDEX

GLOSSARY

biome (BUY-ome)—an area with a particular type of climate, and certain plants and animals that live there

carbon dioxide (KAHR-buhn dye-AHK-side)—a colorless, odorless gas that people and animals breathe out

community (kuh-MYOO-nuh-tee)—populations of people, plants, or animals that live together in the same area and depend on each other

ecology (ee-KOL-uh-jee)—the study of the relationships between plants and animals in their environments

environment (en-VYE-ruhn-muhnt)—the natural world of the land, water, and air

mate (MATE)—to join together for breeding

offspring (OFF-spring)—animals born to a set of parents

organism (OR-guh-niz-uhm)—a living plant or animal

population (pop-yuh-LAY-shuhn)—a group of people, animals, or plants living in a certain place

recycle (ree-SYE-kuhl)—the process of turning something old into something new

transpiration (transs-puh-RAY-shuhn)—the process by which plants give off moisture into the atmosphere

READ MORE

Bjorklund, Ruth. *24 Hours in a Grassland*. A Day in an Ecosystem. New York: Cavendish Square Publishing, 2018.

Rice, William. *Life and Non-Life in an Ecosystem*. Huntington Beach, CA.: Teacher Created Materials, 2016.

Rodger, Ellen. *Artic Research Journal*. Ecosystems Research Journal. New York: Crabtree Publishing Company, 2018.

Watts, Pam. *Ocean Ecosystems*. Ecosystems of the World. Minneapolis, Minnesota: Core Library, an Imprint of Abdo Publishing, 2016.

INTERNET SITES

Use Facthound to find Internet sites related to this book.

Visit *www.facthound.com*

Just type in 9781543529463 and go!

 Check out projects, games and lots more at
www.capstonekids.com

INDEX